NURSERY RHYMES REIMAGINED

FARM, FAMILY, NEIGHBORS, AND COMMUNITY

DENISE MASTEN

Nursery Rhymes Reimagined
Farm, Family, Neighbors, and Community

Written By: Denise Masten
Book Designed and Edited By: Aaron C. Butler

ISBN: 9781967082353 (Paperback)
ISBN: 9781967082360 (eBook)

Library of Congress Control Number: 2025909513

Printed in the United States of America

BookButler Publishing Company
Upper Marlboro, MD 20774

TheBookButler.com

BookButler Publishing Company titles may be purchased in bulk for educational, business, fundraising, or sales promotional use. For information, please email:
info@thebookbutler.com

FORWORD

Remember when you were younger, when the world was a canvas of imagination? The days began with the aroma of nap time at school and dissolved with bedtime's sweet embrace. These moments were often accompanied by the soothing rhythms of nursery rhymes, recited by caregivers, parents, and teachers... their breath releasing the fragrance of bubble gum, butterscotch, peppermint, relaxation, security, or orange Tic-Tac. But as I grew older and my own family began to bud, I reflected on those familiar verses. The whimsical tales that once rocked me tightly to sleep now seem to carry an unsettling fear, as if the shadows of their meanings were hidden in the dark of a partially opened closet.

My ah-ha moment sparked a creative journey in me—a drive to reimagine these trigger stories in more positive thought and infuse them with a modern twist that resonates with today's communities. In these pages, you'll find familiarity and similarities, but with narratives that reflect contemporary themes, challenges, and triumphs. The aim is not to rid those stories but to expand their angles, to breathe new life into them while respecting their origins.

Join me as I embark on this whimsical adventure, where nursery rhymes meet the realities of modern life. Together, we'll uncover the layers of meaning hidden within these tales and perhaps, in the process, find a little magic that still lingers in the air, ready to open the doors of our minds into a new kind of dream. Welcome to a reimagined world of nursery rhymes–where the past meets the present, and every story has a twist waiting to be discovered.

TABLE OF CONTENTS

Chapter 1
Living in Bales and Logs...................... 4

Chapter 2
Rockin My Baby.............................. 16

Chapter 3
Shelby's Commute 30

Chapter 4
Shoes Everywhere Foster Care 38

Chapter 5
BnB Delivery................................. 44

Chapter 6
Blu Rhythm Dreams·························· 52

About the Author ························· 59

CHAPTER 1

LIVING IN BALES AND LOGS

"Welcome to the B&L, where we break it down fuh ya and keep it real wit chuh! Chile, did you think that those nursery rhymes you listened to were sweet little bedtime stories? Honey, you ain't heard about what really went down all over town. Don't worry though, I got you; I've got the tea–straight from Willy Winkle's mouth (literally, that boy can't keep a secret)."

"Sort of strange, though, how much he actually pays attention, with him being socially awkward and all. I mean, I can't tell sometimes with all the running through town that he does, knocking on people's doors and such. Tap tap taddap tap tap tap. Welp, (it's time for the percolator) speak of the percolating tea kettle. That's him! I know that knock anywhere. (Muffet looks between the open spaces of her vertical blinds)"

"Look at him, bless his heart; he's been doing the same old dance since he was in middle school...out there just skipping like it's no one's business. It's a dang shame how he swallowed those flies that got in his buttermilk. I guess he just couldn't shew them away fast enough. Poor darlin always has to skip right to the lou before he starts talking. Anywho (whispering), let's go grab a snack because he's about to chat and tell us what's really been going on around here..."

It was about that time of year! Yep, a time when our families, far and near, came together and celebrated the harvest with fellowship, food, and fun. The Bales and Logs community was getting ready for the B&L Annual Fall Festivus. One of the largest turnouts for the Festivus is for the Tooth Fairy's contest with guaranteed cash prizes.

Yes, sir, when I tell you Red Hood's Grandma's pastries are sticky fingers good, 'they will have a wolf stalk you in the woods and hide wearing granny's duster' type of good! During last year's event, Dumpty's kid mauled his way through those pastries in under 3 minutes! I cannot wait to see who will claim the trophy this year!

Now, it would be really nice if all of the three piglet brothers could, for once, come together long enough to be a part of the Open House tour. The tour is simply one of the most beautiful sights to see during the Fall. To visually experience how some people can be so creative with red clay.

Unfortunately, but fortunately for two of the brothers, their straw and wood houses can be updated to aluminum siding, per the huff and puff safety mandates that were put into effect nine months ago. But, as usual, neither of the two attended the monthly B&L Hall meeting at the Barn. Had they attended, they could have addressed the O&S (oinks and squeaks) they may have had about their frequent vandalism experiences.

It would have also given them plenty of time to apply and get approved for disaster relief through the Habitat for Animalty. Anywho, I do know why the pig brothers didn't show up. I mean, I am the founder and president of the town's "B&L CWA...Community Watch Association." It's a nosey job, but...I meant to say that since I am so observant and live up on a hill with the perfect view of the entire neighborhood, I am obviously the only perfect candidate.

While trying to eat my morning bowl of cream of wheat, I saw pigs fighting in their pen and oinking over slop portions and the last wolf incident. I saw mud flying everywhere, pig feet in the air, and the type of pig latin the two of them were using was not for young piglet ears, let me say! I didn't see the entire thing, though, because somebody's pet 🕷 came and sat down beside me to watch the fight, I reckon.

But this Muffet has arachnophobia, so pig-tailing my rump off that rock and scurrying in the house, I was able to peep the tail end of the altercation from the window! It makes no sense how some think they can still huff and puff puff pass their way through life.

Mm hmm, Wolf bully, you can't keep a pig down with all that emphysema coughing and those balding gray chinny chin chin hairs! When will those three pigs get together and just mud wrestle your false fangs?

Tighten up that denture grip and sleep with your good eye open.

CHAPTER 2

ROCKIN MY BABY

Before I get into this Rock-a-bye Baby "story," let me tell you I'm providing some context for the words I have recited for years... Rock-a-bye Baby on the treetop. Can you say scary 👣? When the wind blows, the cradle will rock. Wait for it...When the bough breaks, the cradle will fall. And down will come baby, cradle and all.

How did we ever become comfortable enough to fall asleep so soundly as children with those words? I had so many unanswered questions growing up, as I am almost sure you may have your own version of the tale I heard. I always wondered how the baby ended up on the treetop in the first place. I mean, who would climb up into a tree with a baby and then leave? Now, in this newly evolved version of Rock-a-bye Baby, the treetop does not exist.

Yes, you heard it correctly! In fact, there is actually a much safer and more positive explanation than an actual treetop with a baby-filled cradle rocking in it while the wind is blowing. The tree is actually a front porch. Whew... Now, that's better! The weight-limited cushioned swing is nestled on the far-right side of the porch, where the bow is the chain, and the cradle is a porch swing. It was nap time, but the baby was fussy, and the new parent couldn't get the baby to settle.

So, the song Rock-a-bye Baby on the front porch. If I rock too hard, you, it, and I will be on the floor. Needless to say, the baby didn't take too much longer to calmingly fall asleep. Now, think about this for a second, as you are feeling sleepier. You are on the front porch, in a cushioned swing, feeling a good breeze on your skin, and the swing is moving back and forth so gently in a similar motion as you are being held ever so securely in comfort.

Try this and let us know! Think about what helps you relax before you go to sleep.

What do you do? What song is sung? What relaxing music is played?

Somebody, Please Rock That Baby?

Ooo, that's a charming little house! On the opposite side of my hill, there lives a family who seems to have been blessed with a "little." Every evening, the dusk of the sun paints it with hues of orange and pink. I love the refreshing feeling of escape through the beautiful feeling that mosquitoes wouldn't be joining in the peaceful view of the eye candy skyline.

The family settles down on the front porch after dinner. The porch, decorated with hanging plants and twinkling lights, ...that's a magical atmosphere after a long but eventful day. I wonder if those plants are real or silk, though.

(Oops) There seems to be one small smidget of a dilemma: the little one gets a bit fussy when it comes to nap time.

Mommy is trying everything–rocking, singing, gently bouncing and even dad decides to showcase his old head dance skills (bwahahaa) –but nothing seems to soothe the little one. Until one day, as the gentle breeze (with the fresh fragrance of chicken house and a hint of skunk of toilet spray) rustles the leaves and the world seems to slow down, the mother has an idea. Instead of singing the old, slightly frightening lullabies, she decides to create a new version entitled "Rock-n-My Baby."

"Rock-n-My Baby on the front porch," the mother sang softly, her voice blended with the sounds of nature. "If I rock too hard, you, it, and I will be on the floor." The words flowed like a gentle stream, and with each line, the vibes in the atmosphere changed.

The cushioned swing creaked softly as it was swinging back and forth, mimicking the warm embrace of a mom and dad's loving presence.

As Mother continues exhaling melodic acoustics, Little's eyelids grow heavier, the rhythmic motion of the swing lulling them into a peaceful slumber. The worries of the day fade away, being replaced by the soothing melody and the warmth of the evening breeze.

Mother and Father smile at Little, feeling a sense of relief washing over both of them. The front porch had transformed into a sanctuary of comfort and safety, far removed from the fearful baby being in a dang treetop of the old tale.

Now, take a moment to imagine yourself on that front porch, feeling the gentle sway of the swing beneath you, and reflect on what helps you unwind before sleep. Do you have a favorite song that echoes in your mind, perhaps a soft lullaby or a calming instrumental piece? Maybe you find solace in the sounds of nature, like the rustling leaves or the distant chirping of crickets.

Whatever it is, allow those soothing thoughts to wrap around you like a warm blanket, guiding you into a restful night's sleep in an interesting dreamland. See, I'm glad I don't take anyone's word for anything
...seeing is believing!

CHAPTER 3

SHELBY'S COMMUTE

In a little part of the town, there lives a group of children who love to gather at the edge of their neighborhood. They would sit on the wall, waiting for the arrival of someone special. This person was known simply as "She," and the children would sing a familiar tune they came up with together, "She'll be coming around the mountain," filled with excitement and anticipation. But as the lamp pole lights began to come on one by one, the children often pinned up with anticipation and a hint of anxiety.

Who was "She?" Did she say what time she was coming? And which bus was she riding on? The mystery of "She" left the children feeling uneasy, as they were not fond of surprises from strangers, so they decided to take matters into their own hands and give "She" a name: Shelby.

Shelby is an education advocate who dedicates her time to providing educational resources to families in the community. The children admire her, not just for her knowledge but for her kindness and the way she always makes learning fun.

As the children sit on the side of the wall, they decide to rewrite the story of Shelby. Instead of waiting in uncertainty, they agree that they want to know exactly when she will arrive. "Shelby's coming across town when she's done!" they sang, their voices ringing with newfound confidence. They knew that she finished her teaching duties at 3 PM, and they could eagerly anticipate her arrival.

As the clock strikes three, the children feel a flutter of excitement in their hearts. They can see Shelby's familiar figure driving toward them in her motorized wheelchair, her smile brightening the evening. She waves enthusiastically, and the children rush to greet her, feeling a sense of trust and joy.

From that day on, the children learn the importance of communication and trust. They understand that surprises can be delightful when they come from someone they know and love. They no longer felt anxious waiting for Shelby; instead, they looked forward to her visits, knowing she would always come across town when she finished her work of the day.

So, close your eyes and prepare for sleep; remember the joy of connecting and the comfort of knowing that those who care for you will be there as often as they are able, just like Shelby coming across town when she gets off from work or runs errands.

Sweet dreams!

CHAPTER 4

SHOES EVERYWHERE FOSTER CARE

An old lady who lived in the shoe...Foster Care/Respite parent whose one-bedroom loft apartment was way too small for the immeasurable amount of children she rescues over time. For breakfast, the old lady would serve the children Old Fashion Oatmeal with a drizzle of 100% pure 🍯, because the flakes are much larger and the honey is sweeter and healthier.

For supper, she would give the children broth to help their immune systems become strong in preparation for the Winter months. Having hot cereals, broths, soups, or stews like vegetables, chicken, or beef, with a sandwich of some kind...like grilled cheese (if you have bread), keeps your insides warm and healthy. Because the old lady frequently had so many children, many times, the old lady did not have bread to give the children.

Sometimes, she did not have enough for all
of them to have a second serving, but she
did not complain. She does, however, keep
enough rectangle dinner crackers and
peppermint tea in the house. The old lady
never had children of her own, so she took
classes at the Department of Social Services
in her community and became a child
advocate and certified
Foster Care / Respite Parent.

She became a safe haven for many children who were alone. The old lady always wanted a closed front porch, and sunroom, and a nice-sized backyard with a privacy fence. With the funds she was receiving, she was able to afford a larger, more comfortable place for herself and the new children she took in.

As for the children, because of the love and nurturing they received, they appreciated the old lady's sacrifices and reciprocated her love, especially after they were old enough to move out on their own and have families.

44

CHAPTER 5

BnB DELIVERY

Bubba Hubbard...(in his bathroom mirror, giving himself a nice clean shave with homemade shaving cream) "Whew, I am so excited about this year's Festivus!" Bubba reminisces about being Quarantined when he caught the newest strain of COVID. If that wasn't enough, his social security check is late yet again.

For those that have to live off of the coins, however few or more some receive, once-a-month income is never enough. Bubba became an empty nester once his children grew up and moved out. His coordination wasn't as good as it used to be, therefore, his doctor wrote him a prescription for a support animal. He needed one that would bark if he needed help from a fall or had an anxiety attack.

With a letter of medical necessity being
written on his behalf to the management
team of his building, he could have a pet in
his unit without paying a pet deposit. He and
his sister thought it would be better if they
shared the family house on what used to be
a beautiful 10 acres, and so they did
until recently.

Usually, he didn't have to be concerned with household and business matters because his sister, Bubbles, handled things.

Bubbles has been in a long-term care rehab facility for quite some time for long-term COVID, and Bubba had to handle his own affairs.

He had little food for himself and his support animal, Pom Pom. Having to choose between paying bills and buying food was difficult. Well, at least that's how the story began. Mr. Hubbard had been thinking for quite some time that he should move to Helping Hands Assisted Living Retirement Community.

One of Mr. Hubbard's new neighbors, who volunteered at a local food pantry, wanted to make sure that he and his pet had plenty of food in the house since he was not able to go out as much as she wanted. So, a neighbor put Mr. Hubbard's name in for a commodities food box at the B&L Day Center.

The neighbor also told Mr. Hubbard about another resource, which is a local farm in their community that will deliver produce on Thursdays weekly. Mr. Hubbard was so relieved to know he and his pet wouldn't have to be without food. He was thankful to God and was able to enjoy the Festivus with high spirits.

CHAPTER 6

BLU RHYTHM DREAMS

My name is Little Boy Blue, and I am a nephew of Mr. and Mrs. Farmer. Have you heard of me? Did you know I play the trumpet? Well, it doesn't matter (yawning), because I'm so very excited to tell you (sleep...2 minutes later). Oops! I apologize; I fell asleep. I have a condition called narcolepsy that makes me fall asleep anytime from about 30 seconds to two minutes, wherever I am. Ok, where was I? Oh, yes, I love my trumpet, and I always get excited about visiting my Aunt and Uncle.

My dad, Jack, has been telling me stories about his Summer visits to his relatives who had a lot of wood and acres of farmland. I overheard my parents talking one night about how they felt the change in scenery and air quality may do me some good. So, my dad called Uncle Farmer, and it seemed like they were on the phone for hours playing catch-up. But as the days went by, at the end of the school year, my parents drove me to Bales and Logs for the Summer.

When we arrived, Uncle and Dell Farmer said, "Hey there, Blue! We want you to meet our son, Jack." He is a little shy at times, so he likes to sit in the corner. "Did you bring your trumpet?" "Yes, Auntie, I always have it with me wherever I go." Well, my parents had a long drive back to the city, so they left. Uncle and Auntie Farmer prepared a delicious meal and talked about farming life. Cousin Jack was told to take me on a tour after dinner, but he left me, so it became a self-guided tour.

Wow! I was so surprised at all the farm animals I saw that I started getting sleepy, so I fixed my eyes 👀 on this pretty little thing called a haystack. Apparently, there was a conversation about my supposedly cow and sheep watcher job description that I wasn't invited to be a part of. What's that? I think I hear someone calling my name, but I'm not answering. I hear nothing, so stop asking me to blow my dang horn! I just got here, and whatever you were doing before I arrived...keep doing it!

The sheep 🐑 🐑 were out grazing in the meadow. The cows 🐄 🐄 were in the corn field. But where was this guy, who knew absolutely nothing about looking after cows and sheep? He is propped up against an oddly cozy-looking haystack, fast asleep counting sheep. Yuh boy was tired 😴!

TO BE CONTINUED

ABOUT THE AUTHOR

As an author, entrepreneur, motivator, and serial educator, Denise Masten is driven by a deep passion for storytelling and a love for bringing smiles to those around her. Through her work, she aims to inspire readers to envision a more positive outlook on life by creating stories that are visually engaging, interactive, and fun. Her goal is for every reader to connect with the stories on a meaningful level and walk away feeling uplifted.

.